AN INTRODUCTION TO
Mass and Weight

3RD GRADE

PHYSICS FOR KIDS
Children's Physics Books

BABY PROFESSOR
EDUCATION KIDS

Speedy Publishing LLC
40 E. Main St. #1156
Newark, DE 19711
www.speedypublishing.com

In this book, we're going to talk about the difference between the mass of an object and the object's weight. So, let's get right to it!

Atoms.

What Is Mass?

All the objects you see around you are made of matter. The matter is made up of different types of atoms. Some atoms are denser than others depending on the types of elements they are. Physicists needed a way to calculate how much mass is in one object compared to another.

How Is Mass Measured?

The standard unit of measure used to measure the mass of larger objects is the kilogram. The kilogram is equivalent to 1,000 grams and it is abbreviated by using the letters kg. Mass is measured using a device called a balance. The mass of the object is compared against known masses to be measured in kilograms or fractions of a kilogram.

Formula of mass or weight.

Mass (WEIGHT)

1 gram (g)	:	1000 mg
1 kilogram (kg)	:	1000 g
1 tonne (t)	:	1000 kg
1 tonne		
1 ounce (oz)	:	437.5 grains
1 pound (lb)	:	16 oz
1 short cwt	:	100 lb
1 long cwt	:	112 lb
1 short ton	:	2000 lb
1 long ton	:	2.240 lb

Physicists have two main ways they measure the mass of an object. The first way is the object's inertial mass and the second way is the object's gravitational mass.

Weight with mass symbol tied on a rope.

Inertial mass

If you had one object that had more mass than the other, which do you think would be easier to push? It seems obvious that the object that had the lesser of the two masses would be easier for you to push. Of course, this assumes that you would try pushing the objects with the same amount of force in each case. This is one way that physicists measure mass, by the way an object resists being accelerated.

Standing Gyroscope.

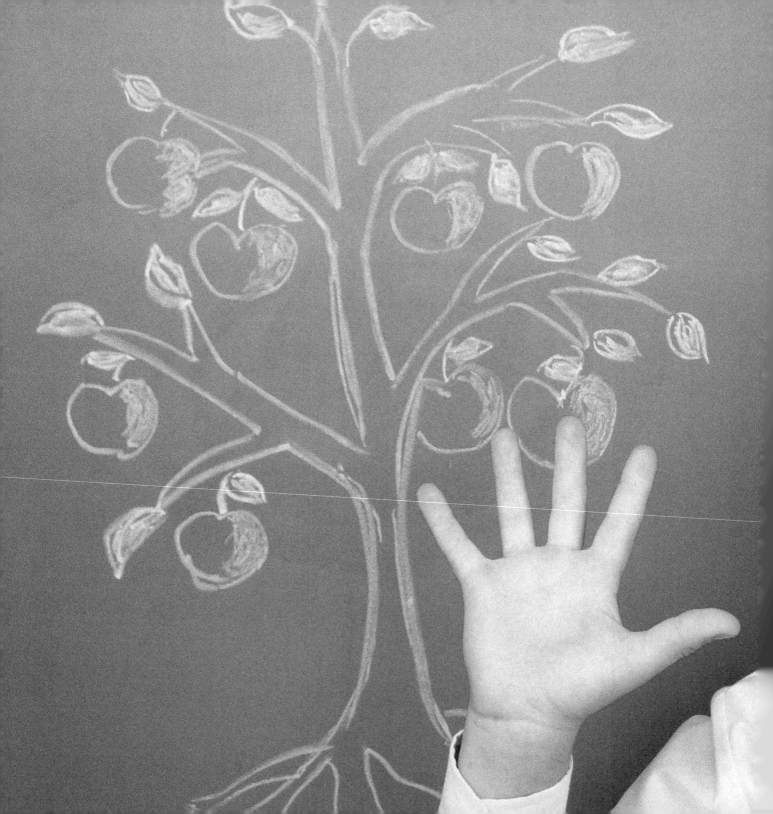

Gravitational Mass

The other way that physicists measure mass is by measuring gravitational mass. This type of measurement can be done in one of two ways. The gravitational mass can be the measurement of how much gravitational pull the object you're measuring has over another object.

It can also be done the opposite way. It can measure the pull another object has on the object you want to measure.

Measuring Small Quantities Of Mass

Sometimes physicists need to measure the mass of molecules, atoms, or subatomic particles. Kilograms wouldn't be a practical way of measuring these very small amounts of mass. The unit of mass used in these types of atomic measurements is represented by *"amu."* This atomic mass unit (amu) is the same as 1/12 of the mass of carbon-12, which is approximately the mass of one of carbon-12's protons.

An apple experiences gravitational fields directed towards every part of the Earth; however, the sum total of these many fields produces a single powerful gravitational field directed towards the Earth's center.

This means that the mass of an atom of carbon-12 is approximately 12 amu. The element of iron has 26 protons and 30 neutrons so its amu is approximately 56 amu. If you divide 56 amu by 12 amu you'll find that the mass of an atom of iron is more than 4.6 times the mass of an atom of carbon-12.

Old-fashioned balance scale.

Mass - unit of measurement.

The Difference Between Mass And Weight

Many people confuse mass and weight. There's a very simple way to keep them straight. An object's mass would never change based on its location. In other words, if you measure a basketball's mass on Earth and then you measure it on Jupiter, its mass, the measure of the matter that exists in that basketball, isn't going to change.

The same thing is true if you measure the mass of a particular atom on Earth or on Saturn. The mass of that atom will remain the same.

However, weight is completely different. Suppose you weigh 100 pounds on Earth. If you stood on Mars, you would weigh a little over 37 pounds and on Jupiter you'd weigh a massive 236 pounds plus a little more! This is because weight is a different type of measurement. It's a measurement that calculated by gravity's force on an object.

On Mars, the gravitational pull is not as strong as it is on Earth so you would weigh less. On Jupiter, the gravitational pull is much stronger than on Earth, so that's why you would weigh much more.

If you've ever seen the video of the United States astronauts on the moon, you'd see the evidence of this. Unlike on Earth, where we really have to work hard to jump up and down, on the moon the gravitational pull is much smaller, so the astronauts weighed a lot less and could bounce around on the surface a lot easier.

Half moon.

Collection of vintage golden and silver calibration weights.

Measuring Weight

When you measure your weight in the morning before you eat breakfast, you jump on a scale and measure your weight in pounds if you're in the US and kilograms in countries where the metric system is used. However, physicists use the measurement of Newtons to describe weight since as we said before, it's a measurement of gravitational force or pull.

ANewton is an international unit of measure. It's named after the famous physicist Isaac Newton. It's the needed force to get an object with a mass of 1 kilogram (kg) accelerating at the rate of 1 meter per second squared in the same direction as the force that was applied to it. The weight of a medium apple is about the weight of a Newton. This is easy to remember because of the legend that Newton discovered the force of gravity when an apple fell from a tree and hit him on the head.

Isaac Newton's apple.

A.

B.

m_1

m_2

y

c

Illustration of the physics principles by which a "Weeble" roly-poly toy operates. A=position of mechanical equilibrium; B=position of mechanical instability; F=gravitational force; y=vertical axis; m1=low-density mass; m2=high-density mass; C=centroid. Note that between positions A. and B. that C raises slightly and becomes off-center.

Converting Mass To Weight

Gravity on our planet can be different depending on where you are standing. However, that difference isn't too significant. It's only about 0.5%. Since the gravity on the surface of the Earth is pretty consistent, weight will also be pretty consistent. That means that we can use a formula to go back and forth from weight to mass or from mass to weight.

The formula you can use is:

Force = Mass x Acceleration

F = ma

This equation comes from Isaac Newton's Second Law. In the equation, **F** is the same as gravity's force measured in Newtons. The variable *m* is the object's mass in kilograms. The variable *a* represents the acceleration that occurs due to Earth's gravity, which is 9.8 meters per second squared.

Newtons law of universal gravitation.

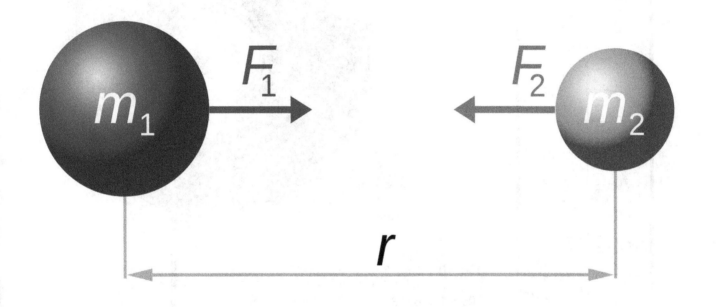

$$F_1 = F_2 = G\frac{m_1 \times m_2}{r^2}$$

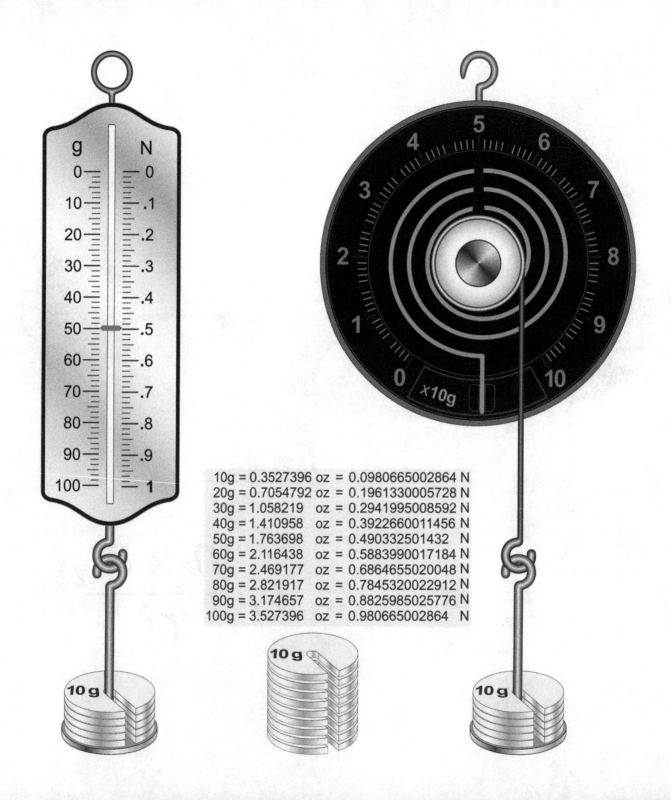

10g = 0.3527396 oz = 0.0980665002864 N
20g = 0.7054792 oz = 0.1961330005728 N
30g = 1.058219 oz = 0.2941995008592 N
40g = 1.410958 oz = 0.3922660011456 N
50g = 1.763698 oz = 0.490332501432 N
60g = 2.116438 oz = 0.5883990017184 N
70g = 2.469177 oz = 0.6864655020048 N
80g = 2.821917 oz = 0.7845320022912 N
90g = 3.174657 oz = 0.8825985025776 N
100g = 3.527396 oz = 0.980665002864 N

When this formula is used to determine the weight from the mass or vice versa, it might be written as:

W = mg

In this form, the variable **W** represents the weight, _m_ represents the object's mass and _g_ is the gravitational acceleration.

Mass and Weight.

Example 1

Problem: What is the weight of an object sitting on the surface of the Earth if its mass is 25.6 kilograms?

Solution: $W = mg$ = (25.6 kg) (9.8 meters per second squared) = 250.88 Newtons

Example 2

If you want to find the mass of an object from its weight you can use the formula $m = \dfrac{W}{a}$.

Problem: What is an object's mass if its weight on the surface of the earth is 3000 N?

Solution: $m = \dfrac{3000 \text{ N}}{9.8 \text{ m/s}^2} = 306.12$ kilograms

Is Mass Equivalent To Size Or Volume?

Mass isn't the same as size and it isn't the same as volume either. The density of the atoms makes a huge difference in the mass of an object. Suppose you had a bottle of soda. Then you dump out the soda and fill it with sand. Next, you dump it out again and this time you fill it with gold coins. Which of these situations would have the most mass?

Gold coins on a grey sand.

It would be much easier to shove the soda across a table than it would be to move the sand. That's because the soda is less dense and has less mass. The sand has more mass than the soda, but the coins have the most mass of all and would be difficult to move. You'd have to use a lot more force.

Old iron scale weights.

The Law Of The Conservation Of Mass

Physics has many fundamental principles. One of its principles is that matter can't be created. It can't be destroyed either. Let's say you had an object that could be put together in pieces in numerous ways. No matter how you put the object together, its mass would remain exactly the same!

Analytical balance.

Old-fashioned balance scale with black tea.

FASCINATING FACTS ABOUT MASS AND WEIGHT

- The word *"Mass"* originates from the word *"Maza"* from the Greek language, which means a *"Clump Of Bread Dough."*

- Physicists believe that all the mass in the visible universe is about 1053 kilograms. That's 10 with 53 zeroes after it!

- If you weigh yourself at sea level, you'll weigh more than you do on the peak of a mountain because you'll be closer to the center of the Earth.

- When you measure the mass of matter in a specific amount of space you're measuring its density. The measurement of density is usually described with grams per cubic centimeter or g/cm^3.

- A metric tonne is the same as 1,000 kilograms.

- Plato, the Greek philosopher stated that weight was the propensity of objects to seek objects that were the same as they were.

- The mass of the Earth is 5.972×10^{24} kilograms.

Awesome! Now you know more about the difference between mass and weight. You can find more Physics books from Baby Professor by searching the website of your favorite book retailer.

Visit

BABY PROFESSOR
EDUCATION KIDS

www.BabyProfessorBooks.com

to download Free Baby Professor eBooks
and view our catalog of new and exciting
Children's Books

CPSIA information can be obtained
at www.ICGtesting.com
Printed in the USA
LVHW060725171222
735213LV00009BA/1164